Amy Roberts

Email: amy@raisingarrows.net

Facebook: http://www.facebook.com/RaisingArrows

Twitter: @raising_arrows

Google+: https://plus.google.com/u/0/+AmyRoberts/posts

Pinterest: http://www.pinterest.com/amyraisingarrows/

YouTube: https://www.youtube.com/user/AmyRaisingArrows

Instagram: https://www.instagram.com/amyraisingarrows

TABLE OF CONTENTS

INTRODUCTION

I've never gotten along with traditional planners. My daytimers have sat empty, my journals unused, my digital planners never printed or filled out. I am in love with the *idea* of planning, but the actual act of planning feels tedious and time-consuming; too much work for the inevitable outcome of never getting to all my plans.

That was how I came to my method of Flexible Homeschool Planning. I needed a "method" that fit me, my family, and our lifestyle. I needed a "method" that didn't take up copious amounts of time and energy, and didn't leave me feeling discouraged about all the plans I didn't get to. I needed to learn to plan on the fly. And I did!

However, for many years I felt guilty about this nontraditional, extremely flexible method I had come up with. Even though it worked, I felt like I wasn't a good homeschool mom if I wasn't using all the pretty planners to plan my entire year and then putting pages into notebooks and folders and crates and setting up elaborate systems that looked neat and organized. It wasn't until a few years ago I realized my system worked, and that fact, in and of itself, made me a "good homeschool mom!"

If you are reading this book, I can almost guarantee you are very similar to me. Traditional methods have not worked (or don't work anymore), and you don't have tons of time to spend on planning. You are looking for a method that is out of the box and works for you and your family. Flexible Homeschool Planning might possibly be the answer to your prayers! In fact, that is MY prayer! If the circumstances you are in as a homeschooling mom are such that you need a method that meets you right where you are, then the method that met (and still meets) my needs, I pray, is the very one YOU need too! May you be blessed by the gift of unstressful homeschool planning!

In Him,
Amy
RaisingArrows.net

CHAPTER 1

Why You Shouldn't Stress About Homeschool Planning

Why You Shouldn't Stress About Homeschool Planning

Let me start with 5 little words that will hopefully change your life...

Homeschool planning should not be stressful.

Now, it might seem counterintuitive considering you are solely responsible for your child's education, but trust me, homeschool planning does not require stress to be doing it right. So, let's dispel that notion right off the bat, so we can take a more objective look at your current homeschool planning method and decide if homeschool planning on the fly will work for you.

Flexible Homeschool Planning might be the perfect plan for you if:

- You always feel behind in your homeschool plans.
- You can't find a planner you can stick with.
- You have started multiple homeschool planners, but never finished any of them.
- You find online homeschool planners to be inaccessible and cumbersome.
- You can't find enough time to do a major planning session.
- You feel like you will "mess up" without extensive planning.
- You feel guilty for not being able to stick with your plans.
- You need flexibility in your homeschool.

When I first started homeschooling, I used a curriculum that had squares of lesson plans all across the page every single day of the week for 36 weeks out of the year. However, nearly every day, I failed (note the word I just used there) to get everything in. I had wisely used the entire summer before my son started his first year of homeschool to plan for the upcoming year. I had printed and cut and laminated for months. I was prepared. But, when I couldn't get everything in every single day, I felt defeated and discouraged. I questioned my ability to properly homeschool my son.

All the planning I had done had gone right out the window within a week or two of starting school. Sometimes it was because a grandparent came to town and took my son out for ice cream, and sometimes it was because it was a rainy day and the project I had on the list was for a sunny day, and sometimes I was just too exhausted to do one more thing. Whatever the reason (excuses are what I often called them), I would have to pencil in that neglected project for another day and hope I could actually fit it in on the new day, crammed between all the other plans I had for that day, which, as you can imagine, only set me up to fail again. Pretty soon, I was weeks behind, and discouraged beyond belief over what I perceived to be my lack of discipline in our homeschooling. I kept resolving to get all of those lessons in, and yet, I kept failing to do so day after day.

But, what I was actually failing to do was to see all that I was getting done in a day and recognize that plans are simply a framework and not the definition of an excellent homeschool education. As Dwight D. Eisenhower said:

Why You Shouldn't Stress About Homeschool Planning

"...I have always found that plans are useless, but planning is indispensable."

In other words, homeschool planning doesn't create a perfect homeschool. *You might want to read that again and soak it in for a second.*

If you are stressed over never getting to all of your plans, it's time to leave that guilt at the door, and embrace a better way. You are not a neglectful homeschool mom if you don't get to all of your plans. You aren't failing at this homeschool thing. You just need a better method. One that allows for flexibility. One that doesn't consistently scream that you are behind. One that doesn't cling so tightly to little square boxes.

But, what about all of those pretty homeschool planners? Aren't they the very definition of good planning? Aren't they the only way to properly plan your homeschool year? Doesn't every good homeschool mom use some sort of planner?

The simple answer is NO.

Planners are not for everyone. No really, I'm serious. Some people's brains don't fit neatly into a spiral bound, boxed-filled, cookie-cutter planner. We are all unique, and for some of us, there is no perfect printed planner. For some of us, there is no perfect digital, fully-customizable planner. For some of us, there is no perfect ANY planner! Consider the possibility that you aren't able to stick with that pretty planner you bought simply

CHAPTER 1

because that planner wasn't made for you! It was made for someone else, and you are now released of the guilty feeling that you *should* have been able to make it work. It wasn't for you in the first place!

The final homeschool planning stressor we need to deal with is time - the stress of not being able to find the time to plan, as well as the stress of not being able to find the time to implement the plans we do manage to make.

I remember feeling inadequate and discouraged that I could not take a weekend away from the family in a hotel room by the seaside to plan out an entire year of our homeschool like my friend Lauren. I was certain those 3 days were the secret sauce to make my homeschool year perfect. Without them, I was doomed to mediocrity and just-getting-by.

At one point in my homeschooling career, I was able to take Sunday nights as a planning time, and I felt like I had finally arrived at the doorstep of homeschool mom greatness. But alas, we moved and the new church we attended had their meetings on Sunday nights. Once again, doomed to mediocrity.

But, let's be honest here - just because I couldn't get 3 days away by myself didn't mean I couldn't have a good homeschool year. And just because Sunday was a church night did not mean that all my homeschool plans were wrecked. I wasn't living fully within my circumstances. I wasn't accepting the life the Lord had given me. I wanted someone else's homeschool planning time, and I was certain someone else's planning plans were my key to success. It's the same concept as thinking the perfect homeschool planner will make all your homeschooling dreams come true. If the planner isn't made for you, it will never work. If the planning time doesn't fit your life, it will never work. It does you no good to fuss about it because no matter how much ruckus you make, it still won't work.

You have only the amount of time you have. If you don't have 3 days in the summer in a hotel, you don't have them. If you don't have Sunday nights, you don't have them. There is no magic, carefully calibrated amount of time that equals the perfect homeschool planning session.

There also isn't a "correct" amount of lesson plans that equal the perfect homeschool plan. You don't get points for planning an entire year of lessons. You aren't going to fail miserably if you don't have homeschool plans written down for Labor Day through Christmas before ever starting in the fall. In fact, I can even promise you that a full month of well-planned-out homeschool lessons will not be enough to shelter you from needing to regroup and revamp at some point during that month.

As far as trying to find the time to implement your plans within your day, I would highly encourage you to recognize that most of the time, not getting all our plans in during the day is entirely OUR FAULT. Yes, this one you are going to have to own up to.

CHAPTER 1

You either put too many things in your day or you weren't flexible enough to realize that you don't have to check all the boxes to have a good homeschool day. Own up to it and move on.

We are going to find a better way to do this homeschool planning thing. For some people, this is not their way. They like the pretty planner or the online tracking software. They have made that method work, and they shouldn't try to reinvent the homeschool planning wheel. But, if you spent this entire chapter nodding your head, then read on, my friend - you and I are kindred spirits.

Why You Shouldn't Stress About Homeschool Planning

CHAPTER 2

What Exactly is Flexible Homeschool Planning?

What Exactly is Flexible Homeschool Planning?

Flexible Homeschool Planning isn't a real method. I just made it up. *(I bet you're really scared now!)* All joking aside, it really isn't a method as much as it is an extension of your life. Homeschool planning has to fit your lifestyle to work. Flexible Homeschool Planning, which is very fluid and natural, lacking a particular shape and definition, is at its very essence, a method that fits your life because it is based on your life.

The final chapter in this book gives you a myriad of ways Flexible Homeschool Planning could be implemented, but ultimately, it has to fit your life. Keep that in mind as you read the rest of this chapter and consider how this could look in your homeschool!

Before we get too much into what Flexible Homeschool Planning IS, let's talk briefly about what it IS NOT. It is NOT:
A long, drawn-out process
A complicated process
A method that takes hours, days, or weeks to complete
A method that has to be done correctly or it won't work

Flexible Homeschool Planning should not take a long time to complete. You should not feel bogged down or overwhelmed by it. There is no "right" way to do it, and you don't need a lot of special paraphernalia to make it work. Flexible Homeschool Planning is literally as simple as you can make it.

That's the second thing you need to keep in mind - DO NOT OVERCOMPLICATE THIS! You will be tempted to think there is no way this can work because it ISN'T hard enough, but don't let yourself go there. Remember that simple can work!

So, let's dive in, shall we?

First, you need to take into consideration all of your curriculum. Do you have workbooks? We'll fit those in. Do you have computer-based curricula? We'll fit that in. Do you have literature-based studies, science, history, geography, music, art? I'll teach you how to make all of those a part of your planning as well. And it won't take you hours to figure out!

In the next chapter, we will discuss how to set up a workflow in your homeschool that helps to take even more stress out of your homeschool planning, but for now, let's just learn the basics of how to Flexible Homeschool Plan.

How Long Does Flexible Homeschool Planning Take?

Flexible Homeschool Planning should take an hour or less out of your week, and even possibly your month, depending on what curriculum you are using and how you are using it. It can be done on a weekend or first thing in the morning or even mid-week after school is finished for the day. Lately, I've been doing my planning on Friday afternoons after our home has been cleaned and the kids are busy getting their weekend started. However, I don't always plan at the same time every week. I know it doesn't take long to do, so I can fit it in wherever and whenever I can. I can also add to it at any time, so it continues to be a work in progress until my next planning session.

What About Workbooks?

If you are using workbooks in your homeschool for any subjects, they are no-brainers. Meaning, you simply do the next thing. Most workbooks are meant to be used every single day in your homeschool, so you know that every single day, your children will be pulling out their workbooks and picking up where they left off. If they did Lesson 21 yesterday, they will do Lesson 22 today. You don't have to plan that!

We use workbooks for math, handwriting, and phonics. I do not plan any of those lessons. They are done first thing in the morning every day after Bible and Read Aloud. I simply move from child to child, helping them through each lesson. I do not do full-blown lectures on these subjects, but rather talk them through new concepts and help them by using the EDGE™ method outlined in the Appendix of this book.

If you have workbooks that have projects that require supplies, consider not doing those projects unless absolutely necessary. If you feel they are necessary, take a quick look through the lessons that will be done that week and jot down supplies needed and anything else you need to gather ahead of time. We will address how to manage those supplies in a later chapter.

CHAPTER 2

What About Computer-Based Curriculum?

Our math (Teaching Textbooks), typing (Typing Tudor), and spelling programs (GradeSpelling.com) are all computer-based. Again, not something that needs to be planned. The children simply pick up where they left off the day before. These types of programs already have structure and do not require you to micromanage them. Check in with your children periodically to see where they are with the lessons and be available if they need help, but there shouldn't be anything required of you in the way of planning for this type of curriculum.

What about Science?

We use Apologia for Science. The text is written to the student. At the beginning of the year, I gather supplies (again, we will talk about how I manage those supplies in a later chapter) and then the text becomes like a workbook - natural progression - done every single day with me checking in on them periodically to make sure they are staying on track.

What about Music & Art?

If your child is taking music lessons, then practicing for those lessons becomes a part of the no-brainer list - just like a workbook. They do it every day during the same workflow as their workbooks and computer-based curriculum.

What Exactly is Flexible Homeschool Planning?

What about Literature & History?

I've lumped these two together because homeschoolers are notorious (us included) for putting these two subjects in the same curriculum, and honestly, I think this is best. Living books on as many corresponding subjects as possible are a great way to teach your children that everything in our universe is intertwined. We use Tapestry of Grace which includes literature, history, geography, and more all in one chronological study.

And THIS is where the planning begins.

How to Plan the Subjects that Need Planning

Many literature-based curricula have pre-filled schedules of some type. Tapestry does not have days of the week, but rather boxes with things to finish for the week - lots of things to finish for the week (not all required). There are other programs that have actual assigned days for each lesson. I want you to ignore these and allow yourself the freedom to do things YOUR way.

Open the lesson plans to the section you will be studying in the upcoming week, grab a pen and paper, and start jotting down the things YOU want to accomplish and the corresponding page numbers, but don't put down any dates. **This is a running list of plans.** If you notice there are supplies you need as you are planning, jot those down on another piece of paper or add them directly to a shopping list or app.

CHAPTER 2

I do this with our preschool curriculum - *A Year of Playing Skillfully* - except on a monthly basis. I take out a piece of paper and write down all of the things I want to do (I do not choose everything!) along with page numbers, and then I add any supplies needed onto my Cozi app so they are ready for me to grab the next time I go shopping.

This running list of activities on a piece of paper is my plan! It is simple. It doesn't tell me when I have to do an activity. It gives me options and flexibility.

A Paradigm Shift

The key to Flexible Homeschool Planning working is allowing yourself to make a drastic paradigm shift. You have to allow yourself to let go of the boxes. The boxes tell you that you must do XYZ on this day or you have failed, or you will have to move XYZ to another day, or you will have to rearrange your entire schedule to fit XYZ in. Homeschool Planning on the Fly tells you that XYZ doesn't have to fall on a certain day to work, and when you find the time to do X, you mark it off the list, leaving Y & Z for another day. This takes the control out of the curriculum's hands and puts it firmly into your hands, removing the stress with it.

Fitting it All Together

Monday you had a stellar homeschool day. The kids got through their work in record time sans meltdowns and temper tantrums. You were able to choose several activities from your running list of plans and passed out everyone's literature for the week.

But on Tuesday, piano lessons outside the house totally derailed you and the kids barely got their regular daily lessons in (remember those workbooks and computer-based studies? - those are your dailies). You were too wiped out to do any of the extra history and geography, but you had already assigned their individual literature assignments on Monday, so you reminded them to take some time to read quietly from their books.

On Wednesday, the heater stopped working and you had to take everyone to your mom's for the morning until the repairman could get there. Rather than start in on the daily work so late in the day, you decided to choose a few easy activities from your running list and keep the day low-key. You also found a couple of neat activities in a magazine at your mom's house that you want to try with the kids, so you write those down and add the needed supplies to your shopping app.

On Thursday, you had another stellar day full of the stuff homeschool dreams are made of. You even got one of those magazine extras in because you already had the supplies on hand for that particular activity.

On Friday, you see that you have several things still on your running list, but some are not as important as you thought they were and some can wait until the next week. You choose a couple to round out your week and call it good.

And THAT is why this is called Flexible Homeschool Planning! You had a plan, but you were able to take each day as it came and decide on that day what you could accomplish, rather than letting a box dictate your plans and potentially crush your day.

Recap of Flexible Homeschool Planning

- Your everyday subjects don't need a lesson plan.
- Anything that does need a plan only takes a pen and paper to accomplish that plan.
- Sit down with curriculum and pen and paper and write out in list form all the things you want to accomplish that week, plus page numbers and supplies needed.
- Gather supplies.
- Let your day dictate how much or how little you accomplish of the plan.
- At the end of the week, assess what can be removed from the plan and what needs to be moved to the next plan.

Now that you understand the basics of Flexible Homeschool Planning, let's put together a workflow to your homeschool day that will really make this plan pop!

What Exactly is Flexible Homeschool Planning?

CHAPTER 3

Setting up a Workflow

Setting up a Workflow

In my humble opinion, Flexible Homeschool Planning works best with a homeschooling workflow in place. Another word for this is a ROUTINE. There should be a routine about your homeschooling day that is predictable. That does not mean it happens every day, but it means that when it happens, it happens in the same order.

Let me give you an example from our homeschool:

The homeschool day starts with Bible Time and a Read Aloud. From there, the older children start their independent subjects as well as their computer-based subjects and literature assignments. The younger children do their workbooks, usually in this order: Handwriting, Math, Phonics. Once all of that is finished, the children taking piano lessons filter through practice time. We eat lunch and then do Tapestry of Grace and preschool projects from *A Year of Playing Skillfully* or other seasonal projects I have found online.

This is our workflow. This has been our routine for years. It is our autopilot. It has been a lifesaver for those months of morning sickness or when I have to be away and Grandma has to get them going on school. And it is what allows me the flexibility to make Flexible Homeschool Planning work.

With a workflow in place, you can easily spot a stellar homeschooling day versus a not-so-stellar one. You can tell if you will be able to accomplish several things on the running list or if you need to ditch the list entirely. A workflow gives you a standard by which to measure your plans.

So, let's get you a workflow!

I prefer to start our day off with Bible Time and a Read Aloud all together in the living room. You could start your day with Bible Time, or a Morning Basket that rotates through a series of books, or a simple seasonal project that gets the creative juices flowing, or even family exercise time that gets the wiggles out right away!

Whatever you choose to start your day with, it needs to qualify as an EVERY DAY thing. As in, you do this particular thing every day. Even a rotating Morning Basket has an every day essence in that you do the Morning Basket itself EVERY DAY (see PamBarnhill.com for more information on the Morning Basket concept).

From there, each child needs a workflow that makes sense to them. For older children, all you need to do is write down all of the subjects they need to accomplish on their own and let them order their own workflow. Eventually, their workflow will become second nature to them.

Note: If you add in a new book or subject, you will have to remind them for a time and possibly write them out a new list of subjects and refer them back to that list often. This list also becomes your checklist for checking up on them periodically.

Setting up a Workflow

For younger children, you guide the workflow. My younger kids all know to do Handwriting first so Mom can take care of a few things before jumping into helping them with school work. Then they do Math, and lastly Phonics because they sometimes have books to read with Mom, and I need that to be the last thing on their morning workflow (apart from Piano practice).

These subjects always occur in the morning prior to lunch. This is so ingrained into our brains that if something happens during our morning hours, we struggle to do this workflow in the afternoon because it just "doesn't feel right."

Our afternoon workflow is where our more flexible plans go - the plans we made using the Flexible Homeschool Planning method! So, for our family that is *Tapestry of Grace, A Year of Playing Skillfully*, See the Light Art, and any fun seasonal projects I find on Pinterest! These are NOT subjects we do every day. These are plans that fit our life! They are done "on the fly."

This is how our family homeschooling routine works, but yours needs to make sense for you. Perhaps you want to do your every day subjects in the afternoon during nap time for your younger children. Or maybe you need to split every day subjects between morning and afternoon hours with the other plans at the very end of the day. The best way to figure out your own family workflow is to take a look at how you naturally do things now. Build your routine on your natural tendencies, and it will work much better for you.

CHAPTER 3

Now that you have a workflow that helps you see what kind of day you are having and better gauge how many of your homeschool plans you can fit in, you are probably beginning to see why I call this Flexible Homeschool Planning. You get to decide what you can handle every single day without boxes and borders! Yay you!

Setting up a Workflow

CHAPTER 4

Tools Needed for Fast Homeschool Planning

Tools Needed for Fast Homeschool Planning

I was tempted to write

Pen
Paper

and let that be it for this chapter, but there are a few other things I'd like you to consider getting that will make this method really sing for you.

Basket or Tote

This is going to be YOUR basket. Call it a Mom's Basket or a Morning Basket or a Homeschool Tote or whatever you want, but this is YOURS and everything you need to manage your homeschool day goes in there.

Here's a peek into my basket to give you an idea of what this might look like. I have a canvas basket with handles that has our Bible story book and current read aloud along with the week's history books. I also have pens and dry erase markers in there, plus our super special pencil sharpener and the rulers that always seem to get lost if I don't keep them in the tote because certain little boys "borrow" them to use as guns.

This Homeschool Tote lends a form of structure to my day. It has everything I need all in one mobile place. Having a spot for my stuff also makes it very handy to be able to tell the children to grab the Bible book and Read Aloud because they know exactly where those are.

I would encourage you to make this basket very much your own. Mine is purple and everyone knows they are not to get into it without express permission from Mom. It does sit on a higher shelf in the dining room, but even if it didn't, they know better than to mess with Mom's basket!

Crate or Shelving System

Your kids need to have a personal space for their school things. While I prefer communal crayons, pencils, scissors and glue, I have found it easier to keep their actual workbooks and other individual assignments separated out. We use open-front stackers that have served this purpose for many years. They are stacked youngest to oldest in a corner in the dining room and fit their workbooks and literature assignments quite nicely. This would also be the place they would keep supplies needed for individual school projects. The older kids keep some of their personal art supplies in there as well. My oldest daughter keeps her school work in a Thirty-One tote near her computer. I do go through these stackers once a month or so to weed out all the extra papers that seem to find their way in there.

Cozi app or other shopping app

I have used Cozi for my shopping for years on the recommendation of a reader. As I make my running list, I add supplies directly into the app so it is ready for me when I'm ready to shop for supplies.

Tools Needed for Fast Homeschool Planning

Pen & Paper

And of course, you need pen and paper. Or a pencil and legal pad. Or your Evernote app. Whatever you prefer to use to take notes and make your planning list. Whatever medium you choose to use to do your homeschool planning, it needs to be something that works FOR you rather than against you. If someone suggested some great app they love and you have been banging your head against a wall trying to make it work for you, QUIT. Do what comes naturally, and if that is pen and paper all the way, then so be it. You aren't behind the times or slow to learn or technologically backward. Embrace the method that works with your unique brain - you will get so much more done!

CHAPTER 5

How to Easily Gather & Store Supplies

How to Easily Gather & Store Supplies

One of the biggest concerns with Flexible Homeschool Planning is that when you decide to do a certain activity, you will not have the supplies you need to do that activity. This chapter addresses that issue and helps you put together a one-stop station for supplies.

First of all, it is imperative that as you do your homeschool planning, you write out a supplies list. Don't rely on your memory or think you will have time to do this later. Every single activity you write down needs to be accounted for. So, if I write down Make Valentine Cards, I need to write down on my supplies list everything I need to do that activity. Often I will just have my Cozi app open and plug those supplies directly into the app.

Before you start complaining that this seems like a lot of extra work, let me explain that you are NOT writing out a list that has every activity and all the supplies needed for that activity. You are simply writing out your running activity list and making sure you have the supplies on hand for that activity whenever you choose to do it. You don't need to know exactly what supplies are for which project - you only need to make sure you have the supplies available so when you decide to do a certain activity, you know you have those supplies on hand.

In our home, these supplies are all kept in a blue laundry basket on a shelf in the dining room where most of our schooling takes place. We call it the "Preschool Basket" because a lot of our projects come from our preschool curriculum, even though everyone in the house likes to do the projects! When I come home from the store with supplies for projects for the month, they all go in that basket so everyone knows exactly where to find the supplies when it comes time to do each activity on the running list. No scrambling for supplies or wondering if someone ate the cereal we were going to sort for the math project. If it belongs to a project, it goes in the basket, and the basket is OFF LIMITS.

You could use a tote with a lid that you keep in the garage or in the basement. You could use a wooden basket kept on top of the bookshelf. You could use tubs in a closet or on a shelf. The possibilities are limited only by the space you have in your home to store your supplies.

And this is where I caution you not to get over-zealous with your running list of projects! Remember when I said you will need to assess at the end of the week or month if you want to drop a project entirely or simply move it to the next week or month? One way to make sure you DO get everything in that you wanted to is to keep your list REASONABLE! This will also keep your budget under control, as well as the amount of supplies you have to store.

I'd also encourage you to make your supplies accessible. If you loathe the thought of going down in the basement to gather the supplies you need for the next project, DO NOT put the tote in the basement! Part of Flexible Homeschool Planning is being able to grab supplies quickly!

How to Easily Gather & Store Supplies

CHAPTER 6

———

Real Life Examples of Flexible Homeschool Planning

Real Life Examples of Flexible Homeschool Planning

This chapter will give you a few real life scenarios of how Flexible Homeschool Planning might look in your home, but remember, this method of planning is as unique as you and your family are! Don't get stuck trying to recreate one of these scenarios, but rather, learn from them and consider how this method would play out with your unique family and circumstances.

Example 1 - Shady Acres Homeschool
Family Dynamic - Dad works a flexible schedule, Mom works from home, all of the children are under the age of 8.

Curriculum - Rod & Staff ABC Series, Five in a Row, random workbooks from a local discount store

Flexible Homeschool Plan - Mom homeschool plans once a week, usually on Sunday night so she can shop for supplies on Monday morning while Dad hangs out with the kids before heading into work that afternoon.

Five in a Row is her only "planned" curriculum, so on Sunday she gathers the book for the week, places it in the FIAR Basket and sits down to look through the curriculum for the activities she wants to do with the kids for that book. She makes her running list and places it in the basket as well. She takes her supplies list and goes through the house gathering things she already has (as long as it isn't perishable) and puts those things into the FIAR Basket and crosses those items off her supplies list. She puts that final supplies list (which has now become her shopping list) in her purse.

On Monday, she buys the supplies she didn't already have on hand. While in the store, she remembers that she wanted to do a baking project with the kids, so she buys the ingredients she needs and jots down a reminder on her piece of paper to add the baking project to her running list, even though it is not a FIAR activity.

When she gets home on Monday, she's too tired to do anything but the Rod & Staff workbooks with the kids. The rest of the day she spends prepping food for the week, playing with the children outside, and reading that week's FIAR book for the first time.

On Tuesday, she starts the day with FIAR as usual. She reads the book again, and does several of the projects. That afternoon the older kids work through their workbooks while the youngers nap. Mom is feeling super productive, Dad is home early from work, and dinner is in the crock pot, so she decides today is a great day for the family baking project. Dad is able to take the toddler outside when he starts to get crazy in the kitchen. The project goes so well, and the kids are begging for more, so Mom decides to sit down that night and look for more easy kitchen projects the kids can do. She adds them to the running list after carefully selecting projects that she already has the ingredients for. However, she also adds a couple that she doesn't have all the ingredients for and puts a star by them so she knows they need to go on next week's plan. She adds

the ingredients to a shopping list and puts the list in her FIAR Basket so it is ready for when she sits down to plan for the next FIAR book.

Wednesday is Dad's long day, so Mom does the normal FIAR lesson and the usual workbooks after lunch, and spends the rest of the day working online and keeping the kids contained.

Thursday, Dad is home until the afternoon, so Mom works online for a couple of hours and then pushes hard to get all of the school work done during the morning hours so she can do the kitchen project with the older kids during naptime.

On Friday, Mom looks over her running list before school time and decides to do just one more FIAR project and call it good. That afternoon, she sees a cute and easy craft online and decides to do it right after workbook time. She writes it down on the running list just so she can cross it off when finished.

And that is a week in the Shady Acres Homeschool! Mom took advantage of Dad being home and her family's naptime schedule to make the most of her homeschool days. She had plenty of flexibility to add and remove projects from her workload and keep her online business running in the in-between hours. Her mornings are full of fun projects to keep little hands busy and her afternoons are fairly steady with plenty of opportunities to throw in a project here and there without wearing herself out.

Example 2 - Heritage Arrows Homeschool
Family Dynamic - Dad travels a lot; Mom has her hands full with a wide range of ages of children.

Curriculum - Many different workbooks and computer-based subjects, My Father's World (used to varying degrees with all of the children)

Flexible Homeschool Plan - Because life is so hectic, Mom typically does her homeschool planning on Monday morning right before she calls the kids in to start the school day. She makes her running list for the week, and puts her list of needed supplies right into her shopping app. She's been at this a while, so her supplies basket is full of goodies from previous lessons and even years.

On Monday, the kids all work through their every day lessons in the morning. Since Mom hasn't picked up any new supplies, she pulls activities and lessons from My Father's World that don't need anything extra. She goes shopping on Monday night for everything she needs for the week.

On Tuesday, Dad is home from a business trip, so no school gets done. Mom knows it is going to be ok since they homeschool year-round and can easily make up for these kinds of special circumstances.

Real Life Examples of Flexible Homeschool Planning

On Wednesday, the kids do their workbook subjects like clockwork, and that afternoon, Mom chooses to do several activities from MFW.

On Thursday, a friend calls with a unique learning opportunity downtown, so after workbook lessons, Mom gathers all the kids in the van and they head to the museum with the rest of the homeschool group for an afternoon of impromptu learning. While there, she finds a book on projects that go along with what they were learning about at the museum and decides to capitalize on the moment. She grabs a couple of things needed for the lesson on her way home and decides they will spend all of Friday reinforcing the wonderful things they learned at the museum the day before.

Friday night, Mom glances at her running list and decides there are enough projects left from the week to just carry the entire list over to the next week. She's not behind. She's actually ahead because her next week is almost entirely planned out already!

Example 3 - Twin Oaks Academy
Family Dynamic - Everyone works together on the family farm. The day begins early and can often be unpredictable. Trips to town are rare, and the family prefers to spend most of their time out of doors.

Curriculum - Eclectic and unit studies based

CHAPTER 6

Flexible Homeschool Plan - Mom plans monthly for her myriad of unit studies and projects. She usually takes the last few days of each month to browse her resources and make plans because the family always takes a trip to town on the first of each month. They rarely go into town any other time. Dad picks up any extras they need when he goes back into town later in the month.

Mom has a big tote for each month's activities, and brings in the next month's tote from the shed as she starts her planning. She first looks through the projects she already has in the tote (sometimes ideas and things she's been collecting for several months and even some leftover items from last year!). She then makes her running list of Unit Studies and Lapbooks and other projects and writes out her supplies list as well. She looks through the tub to make sure she has enough supplies on hand for the projects she did last year and then looks through her house for other supplies on her list. Anything extra she needs, she puts on her shopping list for the 1st of the month.

When she gets home from the big shopping trip, she puts the homeschool supplies for the month in the tote and takes the next day to tidy and sort everything in the tote so she can easily find each unit study and project. She also makes a mental note of which unit study she wants to start with.

Throughout the month, she fits in various projects and unit studies in the afternoons and evenings after chores. Their workflow consists of Unit Studies or other projects, followed by Bible study as a family and a read aloud before bed. The children all have various books they read on their own time. When Mom has a new reader, she works with him or her right after chores in the morning, but this year, everyone who is old enough is reading well on their own, so she simply checks up with their independent reading from time to time.

Example 4 - Lighthouse Academy Homeschool

Family Dynamic - Dad works 9-5, Mom has several health issues that flare up from time to time, the children are all above the age of 10.

Curriculum - Mostly computer-based, but Mom has a creative side that desires to do special projects with the kids when she feels well enough to do so.

Flexible Homeschool Plan - Every month, Mom puts together a list of theme based activities that don't require a lot of extra or expensive supplies. She sends a list of things she needs to her husband via email and he grabs them after work, or she orders supplies online so they come straight to her door. She keeps her list of ideas on the computer and her supplies in a closet in the hallway.

Most days, the kids simply start in on their computer work with Mom checking in on them and helping as needed. Since she never knows when pain may keep her from doing an activity she has planned, she never makes set plans until the afternoon of each day. If she's having a good day, she gathers everyone

CHAPTER 6

around the table or outside or they jump in the car for an impromptu field trip. She tries to take advantage of seasonal activities and projects, and keeps easy projects on hand to enjoy with the children. Sometimes the children even ask if they can put together a project on their own. Mom is always delighted to see how creative the kids can be even when she's not there to guide the activity.

Real Life Examples of Flexible Homeschool Planning

APPENDIX

―――――

EDGE™ Method for Homeschoolers

EDGE™ Method for Homeschoolers

As a busy homeschool mom, the best thing you can do for yourself and your homeschool is to teach your children to work independently. In our family, we have adopted the EDGE™ Method commonly used in the Boy Scouts of America. The acronym stands for:

E = Explain
D = Demonstrate
G = Guide
E = Enable

As mentioned in one of the earlier chapters of this book, I do not lecture through the children's workbooks. I use the EDGE™ Method to gently guide them toward independence with their lessons so that by the time they are in Jr. High, they rarely need my help with their every day lessons (the ones that are part of the workflow).

Let me give you an idea of how the EDGE™ Method plays out in a homeschool setting using a Math workbook as our example.

Math workbooks typically have a new concept introduced at the beginning of the page, followed by a review of concepts learned in past lessons. This is perfect for teaching your children to work independently!

First, EXPLAIN any new material to the child. This may be done using the Teacher's Notes or by simply reading the instructions to your child or better yet, by giving your child a quick explanation in your own words. For instance, suppose your son is learning to measure with a ruler. You would discuss the marks on the ruler and how to measure objects and what unit you will be measuring in. Keep the lesson short and concise.

Next, you demonstrate how to line the ruler up to the line he is measuring in his workbook and show him how to read the ruler and where to write his answer. This is the DEMONSTRATE part of the method. This is very brief. I usually only do 1-2 problems for my child before moving to the next letter in our acronym.

GUIDE - Once you have explained and demonstrated, you want him to take over and begin to have ownership of the new material he is learning. However, he needs you to be there to make sure he is doing it correctly. This wards off any major mistakes in how he is solving problems and gives him the confidence to try on his own, knowing you are there to guide him in the right direction. As soon as you see he understands the concept, it is time to...

ENABLE. This is the most difficult stage for the homeschool mom AND the homeschooled child. You may be tempted to micromanage his work so you know he is doing it correctly, and he may be tempted to avoid trying on his own (and possibly failing) in favor of begging you to help him. So, the key to this part of the method actually working and leading to an independent learning process is that YOU MUST LEAVE.

EDGE™ Method for Homeschoolers

As soon as you see that he understands the concept (even if he tries to convince you otherwise), you have to walk away and let him try. Reassure your child that he can do this and that you will be back to check in on him, but walk away! Also instruct your child to move on to the rest of the lesson on the worksheet because he already knows that material.

I am usually only away from the child's side a few minutes as I walk around to check on the other children, but it is enough for that child to understand that I expect him to work on his own.

Implementing the EDGE™ Method in your homeschool is an extremely important tool to creating a workflow to your homeschool day that doesn't bog you down and allows you to maximize your time with ALL of your children, rather than being monopolized by one child.

Please, keep in mind that some children will need more of a certain piece of the acronym than others. Some children need more explaining, while others need more guidance. Ultimately, your goal is children who can learn on their own, and this can only be fostered in an environment where parents believe in their children and allow them to try and fail without judgement.

Made in the USA
Columbia, SC
02 September 2021